People in History

Written by Fiona Macdonald
Illustrated by Martin Salisbury

First published in Great Britain in 1998 by
Dempsey Parr
13 Whiteladies Road
Clifton
Bristol
BS8 1PB

ISBN: 1-84084-204-0

Printed in Spain

Produced by Miles Kelly Publishing Ltd
Unit 11
Bardfield Centre
Great Bardfield
Essex
CM7 4SL

Designer: Diane Clouting
Editor: Linda Sonntag
Artwork commissioning: Branka Surla
Project manager: Margaret Berrill
Editorial Assistant: Lynne French
with additional help from Jenni Cozens and Pat Crisp

Contents

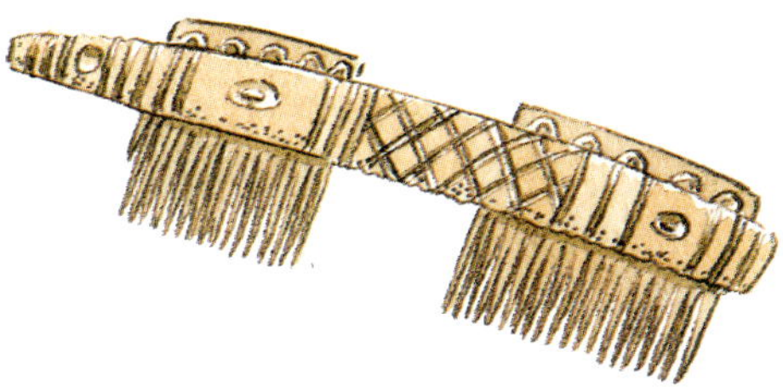

Ice Age home

This tent is made with the skin and bones of the woolly mammoth.

Who walked to America?

THE FIRST AMERICANS! FOR MILLIONS OF YEARS, NORTH AND SOUTH AMERICA were cut off from the world by deep, stormy oceans. No one lived there. Then, during the last Ice Age, the oceans froze and parts of the sea-bed were uncovered. A 'land-bridge' of dry sea-bed linked America and Northeast Asia. Many wild animals lived on the land-bridge, so groups of hunters roamed across it in search of food. Eventually, they reached America, and settled there. Historians are not sure exactly when this happened, but it was probably about 18,000 years ago.

Who lived in huts made of bones?
Groups of nomads who lived on the plains of Eastern Europe about 15,000 years ago. They hunted woolly mammoths, ate the meat, and made shelters from the skin and bones.

Did people live in caves?
Yes, but not all the time. Nomad hunters built temporary shelters in cave entrances and used inner caves as stores. On hunting expeditions they camped in shelters made of branches, brushwood, dry grass and bracken.

What were the first houses like?
Small, single-storey and made of sun-dried mud. They were built in Middle Eastern lands around 11,000 years ago. The first villages were built close to streams and ponds, to ensure a steady water supply.

When did people start to live in towns?
Jericho in Jordan (built around 10,000 years ago) and Çatal Hüyük in Turkey (built around 8,000 years ago) are the world's first big towns. They were centres of trade and craftwork, and were surrounded by strong walls.

What did prehistoric people wear?
In cold countries, they wore leggings and tunics made from furs and skins, sewn together using bone needles and sinews for thread. In hot countries, they wore skin loincloths – or nothing at all!

Hungry nomads set out from Siberia on the long trek to America.

Ape: Australopithecus

This early human ancestor lived about 3 million years ago.

Hominid: Homo habilis

The first toolmaker lived about 2 million years ago.

Human: Homo sapiens sapiens

Modern men and women first developed around 200,000 years ago.

How did modern humans develop?

OUR DISTANT ANCESTORS ARE A GROUP OF ANIMALS KNOWN AS PRIMATES. Primates first appeared on earth about 50 million years ago, and looked rather like squirrels. Over millions of years they changed and grew, as the environment changed around them and they learned new skills to adapt to it. Slowly, they developed into apes, then into hominids (almost-humans), then into modern human beings.

How do we know about apes who lived millions of years ago?
From fossil remains. Fossils are made when chemicals in the soil soak into dead bodies and turn the bones to stone. After many years, the soil turns into rock with fossils hidden inside.

Where were the first farms?
In the Middle East. About 11,000 years ago, people there noticed that wild grains they had accidentally scattered on the ground sprouted and grew into plants. So they cleared plots of land, scattered more grain, and harvested it when it was ripe.

The first Americans

Who were the Neanderthals?
A type of human who lived in Europe and Asia from around 200,000 to 35,000 years ago. Neanderthals were short and stocky with low, ridged brows. They died out – no one knows why – and were replaced by modern humans, who originated in Africa.

When did people start to read and write?
About 6,000 years ago. The Sumerians (who lived in present-day Iraq) were the first people to invent writing. They used little picture-symbols scratched on to tablets of soft clay. Only specially trained scribes could read them.

What did the first Americans carry with them?
Everything they needed to survive – spears and nets for hunting; seeds, berries and dried meat to eat; furs to use as cloaks or blankets, and skin coverings for tents.

Where are the pyramids?
In Egypt, in North Africa. They stand on the west bank of the River Nile. The Egyptians believed this was the land of the dead, because the Sun set there. They built their homes on the east bank of the river – the land of sunrise and living things.

How old are the pyramids?
The first true pyramid was built around 2575 BC. Before then, people were buried under flat-topped mounds, called 'mastabas', and in pyramids with stepped sides. The last pyramid was built around 1570 BC.

What were Egyptian houses like?
Small and simple, with flat roofs that served as extra rooms and courtyards where people worked. Rich people's homes were large and richly decorated, with fine furniture, gardens and pools.

How was a pyramid built?
By man-power! Thousands of labourers worked in the hot sun to clear the site, lay the foundations, drag building stone from the quarry, and lift it into place. Most of the labourers were ordinary farmers, who worked as builders to pay their taxes. Expert craftsmen cut the building stone into blocks and fitted them carefully together.

What are the pyramids made of?
Of hard, smooth limestone. Top quality stone was used for the outer casing; poor quality stone and rubble were used for the inner core.

Why were the pyramids built?

THE PYRAMIDS ARE HUGE MONUMENTAL TOMBS FOR PHARAOHS AND NOBILITY. The Egyptians believed that dead people's spirits could live on after death if their bodies were carefully preserved. It was specially important to preserve the bodies of dead pharaohs (Egyptian kings) and other nobles. Their spirits would help the kingdom of Egypt to survive. So they made dead bodies into mummies, and buried them in these splendid tombs along with clothes, jewels and models of everything they would need in life after death.

A pyramid's shape was important. It represented the rays of the Sun. The Egyptians believed that dead pharaohs were carried to heaven by the Sun's rays.

Were all corpses mummified?

NO, BECAUSE MAKING A MUMMY WAS A COMPLICATED AND EXPENSIVE PROCESS. First, soft, internal organs like the stomach, lungs and brain were removed, then the body was packed in natron (soda) for 40 days to dry out. Finally, it was wrapped in resin-soaked linen bandages, and placed in a beautifully decorated coffin. Most ordinary people were buried in simple coffins made of reeds, or sometimes just in shallow graves in the desert.

Egyptian coffin

The beautifully painted coffin protects the fragile mummy inside. Often, coffins were decorated with portraits of the dead person they contained.

Carved scarab

Why did Egyptian people carry carved stone scarabs?

Scarabs (dung-beetles) collected animal dung and rolled it into little balls. To the Egyptians, these dung balls looked like the life-giving Sun, so they hoped that scarabs would bring them long life.

How many different boats might you see on the Nile?

Rafts made from papyrus reed, flat-bottomed punts, big, heavy cargo boats, splendid royal barges, and funeral boats carrying bodies across the river to pyramid tombs.

Why was the River Nile so important?

Because Egypt got hardly any rain. But every year the Nile flooded the fields along its banks, bringing fresh water and rich black silt, which helped crops grow. Farmers dug irrigation channels to carry water to distant fields.

Did the Greeks invent money?
No. The first coins were made in Lydia (part of present-day Turkey) around 600 BC. But the Greeks soon copied the Lydians and made coins of their own.

The owl was the symbol of the city of Athens.

Greek coins

What were the original Olympic sports?
At first, running was the only sport. Later, boxing, wrestling, chariot races, horse races and pentathlon (running, wrestling, long-jump, discus and javelin) were added. There were also music, poetry and drama competitions.

What were Greek coins made of?
Silver and gold. They were decorated with symbols of the cities where they were made, or with portraits of heroes and gods.

Could women take part in the Olympic Games?
No. Women were banned from the whole site during the games. But once every four years, there were special games for women only. They were held in honour of Hera, wife of the god Zeus.

Did the Greeks go to war?
Yes. In 490 BC and 479 BC, the Greeks defeated Persian invaders, on land and at sea. From 431 BC to 362 BC, there were many civil wars. In 338 BC, Greece was conquered by the Macedonians, and Greek power ended.

Why did the Greeks build so many temples?

BECAUSE THEY WORSHIPPED SO MANY DIFFERENT GODDESSES AND GODS!
The Greeks believed each god and goddess needed a home where their spirit could live. So they built splendid temples to house them, with beautiful statues inside. Each god and goddess had special powers, which visitors to the temple prayed for. Zeus was the god of the sky, Ares the god of war, and Aphrodite the goddess of love.

Were there games in other Greek cities?
Yes. There were over 200 different sports festivals in Greece and the lands round the Mediterranean Sea.

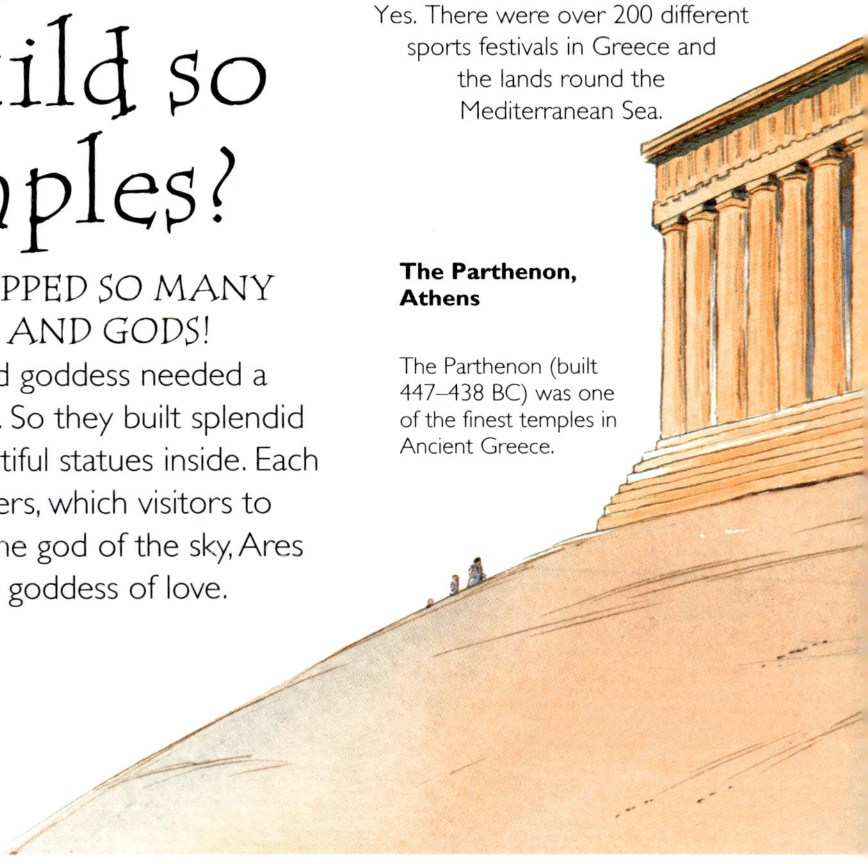

The Parthenon, Athens

The Parthenon (built 447–438 BC) was one of the finest temples in Ancient Greece.

Why did Greek temples have so many columns?
Because their design was copied from ancient Greek royal palaces, which had lots of wooden pillars to hold up the roof.

The original Olympic Games

Who were the Barbarians?
Foreigners – people who did not speak Greek. The Greeks thought their words sounded like 'baa, baa'.

What took place outside temples?
Sacrifices. Animals and birds were killed and burnt on altars outside temples as offerings to the gods. People also made offerings of wine, called 'libations'.

What were Greek warships like?

LONG, NARROW AND FAST. THEY HAD A SHARP BATTERING RAM AT THE PROW, and were powered by 170 oarsmen and huge square linen sails. Sea battles were fought by ships smashing into one another, or by sailing close enough for men to jump across and fight on deck with swords and spears.

The Parthenon was dedicated to the goddess Athene.

After a sacrifice, priests gave portions of roasted meat from the altar to worshippers. They left the fat and bones for the gods!

Who wanted to rule the world?

ABOUT 400 BC THE ROMANS SET OUT TO CONQUER THEIR ITALIAN NEIGHBOURS. By 272 BC they controlled all of Italy – but they didn't stop there! After defeating their rivals in Carthage (Northwest Africa), they invaded lands all around the Mediterranean Sea. In 31 BC they conquered the ancient kingdom of Egypt. They invaded Britain in 55–54 BC. By AD 117, in Emperor Trajan's reign, the mighty Roman Empire stretched from Scotland to Syria and to Iraq.

Who joined the Roman army?
Young men from all over the empire. Recruits had to be fit, tall and strong, aged under 25, and (preferably) able to read and write. Roman citizens became legionary (regular) soldiers. Men from other nations enrolled as auxiliary (helper) troops.

What did Roman soldiers wear?
A uniform designed to keep them safe and warm: armour made of metal strips over a wool or linen tunic, tough leather sandals, a thick cloak, a padded leather helmet, and short trousers or woollen underpants.

How long did Roman soldiers serve?
For about 25 years. After that, they retired. They were given a lump sum of money, or a pension, and a certificate recording their service.

Who attacked Rome with elephants?
General Hannibal, leader of the Carthaginians, who lived in North Africa. In 218 BC he led a large army, including war-elephants, through Spain and across the Alps to attack Rome.

Roman centurion

Centurions were senior army officers. They dressed for parade in a beautifully decorated metal breastplate and a helmet topped with a crest of horsehair.

Why did the Romans spend so long in the bath?
Because Roman baths were great places to relax and meet your friends. Most big towns had public bath-houses, with steam baths, hot and cold swimming pools, sports facilities and well trained slaves giving massages and beauty treatments.

How else did the Romans relax?
By eating and drinking in taverns, gambling, going to the theatre, and watching chariot races and gladiator fights.

Romans rubbed oil on to their skin, then scraped the oil and the dirt off with metal strigils (scrapers) before getting into the bath.

Olive oil jar and strigils

Did the Romans have central heating?
Yes. They invented a system called the 'hypocaust'. Hot air, heated by a wood-burning furnace, was circulated through brick-lined pipes underneath the floor.

Were the Romans expert engineers?
Yes – among the best in the world! They built roads, bridges, aqueducts (raised channels to carry water), long networks of drains and sewers, and the first-ever blocks of flats.

Where did Roman soldiers live?
In goatskin tents, while on the march, or in big barrack blocks inside strongly built forts. Groups of eight ordinary soldiers shared a single room, fitted with bunk beds. Centurions (officers) had a room of their own.

Why did Hadrian build a wall?

TO MARK THE FRONTIERS OF THE ROMAN EMPIRE AND GUARD THEM FROM ATTACK.
Roman emperor Hadrian (ruled AD117–138) made many visits to frontier provinces, such as England, to inspect the defences and to encourage the Roman troops stationed there. The Roman Empire reached its greatest size during his reign.

How long did Roman power last?
The Romans first became powerful around 200 BC. By 100 AD, they ruled a very large empire. Roman power collapsed after the city of Rome was attacked by warlike tribesmen from Asia around 500–400 BC.

Hadrian's Wall in the north of England is 120 km (75 miles) long. Roman soldiers patrolled the wall, looking out for Celtic raiders. The Celts wore checked trousers, or went into battle naked, after painting their bodies blue.

Hadrian's Wall

When were the Vikings powerful?
Viking raiders first sailed south to attack the rest of Europe around AD 800. They continued raiding until around AD 1100.

What were Viking ships made of?
Narrow, flexible strips of wood, fixed to a solid wooden backbone called a keel. Viking warships were long and narrow, and could sail very fast. They were powered by men rowing, or by the wind trapped in big square sails.

Where were the Viking homelands?
The countries we call Scandinavia today – Norway, Sweden and Denmark. The word Viking comes from the old Scandinavian word vik, which means a narrow bay beside the sea. That's where the Vikings lurked, ready to set off on raids.

Viking brooch

What did the Vikings seize on their raids?
All kinds of treasure. Churches were a favourite target for attack, because they were full of gold crosses and holy books covered with jewels. The Vikings also attacked farms and villages, and kidnapped the people to sell as slaves.

Who were the raiders from the sea?

VIKINGS! BOLD, BRAVE, BLOODTHIRSTY WARRIORS WHO TERRORIZED ALL THE PEOPLE OF EUROPE. The Vikings made raids from Scotland to Italy, killing, burning and carrying away all they could. It was hard to make a living in the cold Viking homelands, so Viking men sailed off to seek adventure, hoping to get rich by raiding wealthier lands. However, not all Vikings were raiders. Many were peaceful hunters and farmers, who spent most of their lives at home.

Viking raiders

Were the Vikings good sailors?
Yes. They sailed for thousands of miles across the icy nothern oceans in small wooden boats that were completely open to the elements. They learned how to navigate by observing shoals of fish, birds in flight, sea currents, waves and stars.

Did the Vikings reach America?
Yes, around 1000 AD. A bold adventurer named Leif Ericsson sailed westwards from Greenland until he reached 'Vinland' (present-day Newfoundland). He built a farmstead there, but quarrelled with the local people, and decided to return home.

Why did the Vikings comb their beards?

Viking comb

The handle of this Viking comb is made from an elk antler.

BECAUSE THEY WANTED TO LOOK GOOD ENOUGH TO ATTRACT GIRLFRIENDS! At home, all Viking people liked to look good and keep clean. They combed their hair and took sauna baths in steam produced by pouring water over red-hot stones. Viking men and women proudly wore the best clothes they could afford. Both sexes liked to wear fine jewellery and eye make-up and painted their cheeks a glowing red.

Who led the Vikings on their raids?
Usually, the most powerful people in Viking society: kings, earls and thegns (landowners). But sometimes, Viking raiders were led by wild law-breakers, who had been expelled from their local community for fighting and causing trouble.

Who helped Viking raiders and settlers?
The Vikings prayed to many different gods. Thor sent thunder and protected craftsmen. Woden was the god of wisdom and war. Kindly goddess Freya gave peace and fruitful crops.

Viking raiders leap from their longboats and rush up the beach to make a surprise attack.

Who were the Incas?
A people who lived high in the Andes mountains of South America (part of present-day Peru). They ruled a mighty empire from AD 1438 to 1532.

How did the Incas keep records of past events?
On bundles of knotted string, called quipus. The pattern of knots formed a secret code, which no one knows how to read today.

What was the Golden Garden?
A courtyard next to the Great Temple in the Incas' capital city of Cuzco. It contained lifesize models of animals and plants, made of real silver and gold. They were offerings to the gods.

Inca gold

Incas gave gold offerings – like this model of a llama – to their gods.

Why were llamas so important?
Because they could survive in the Incas' mountain homeland, over 3,000 metres (10,000 ft) above sea level. It was cold and windy there, and few plants grew. The Incas wove clothes and blankets from llamas' soft, warm fleece, and used llamas to carry heavy loads up steep mountain paths.

Who spat into their beer?
Inca women. They made a special beer, called chicha, by chewing maize to a pulp, spitting it out into big jars, mixing it with water and leaving it to ferment.

Who was the 'Son of the Sun'?
The Inca ruler – a king who was worshipped and feared. The Inca people believed he was descended from Inti, the Sun god. The greatest Inca leader was Pachachuti Yupanqui (ruled 1438–1471), who conquered many neighbouring lands.

Who climbed up stairways to gaze at the stars?

PRIESTS AND SCRIBES BELONGING TO THE MAYA CIVILIZATION, which was powerful in Central America between around 200 and 900 AD. They built huge, step-sided pyramids, with temples and observatories on top. The Mayans were expert astronomers and mathematicians. They worked out very accurate calendars, and invented a system of numbers using just three symbols – shells, bars and dots.

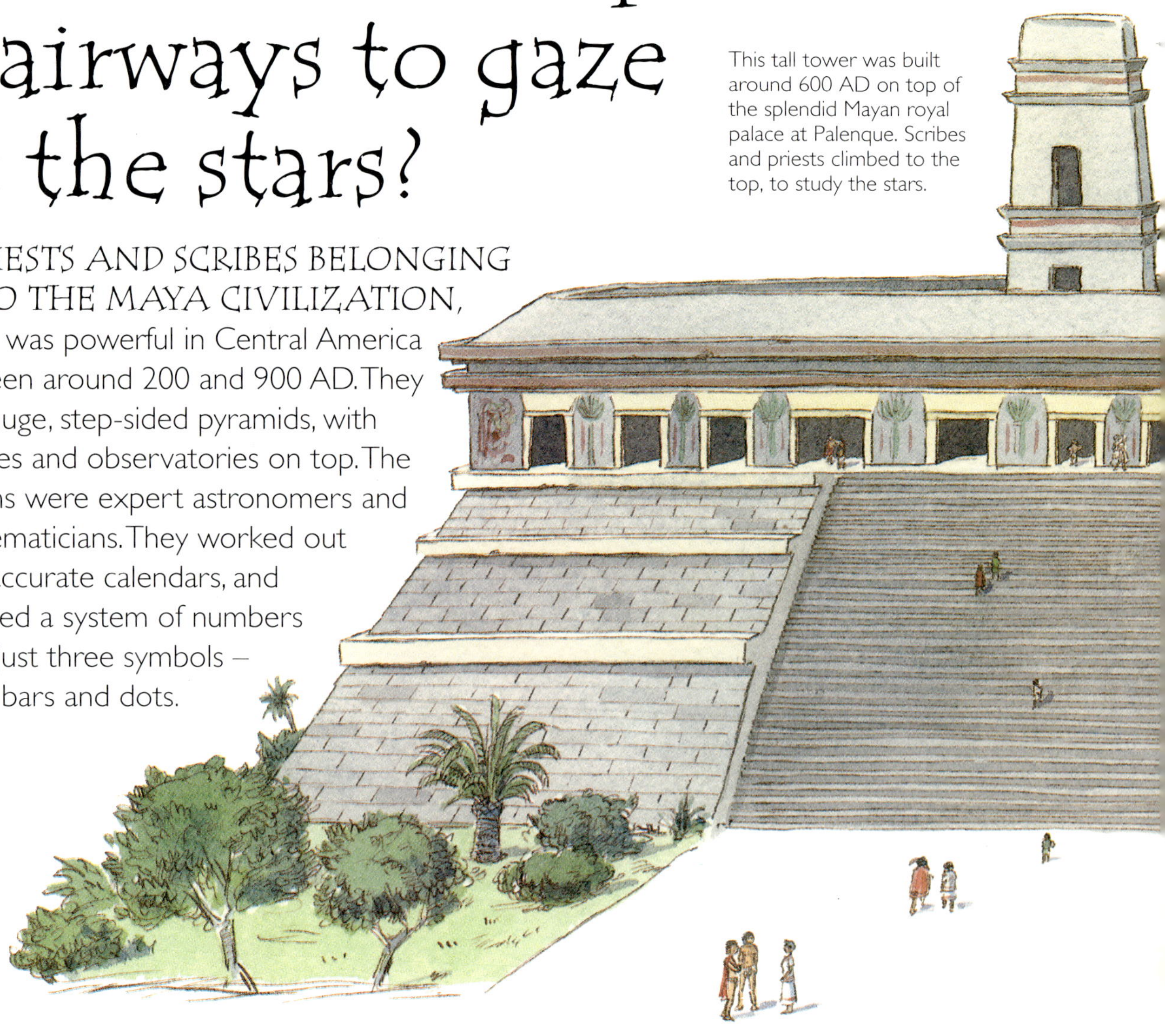

This tall tower was built around 600 AD on top of the splendid Mayan royal palace at Palenque. Scribes and priests climbed to the top, to study the stars.

What was a huaca?
An Inca holy place. Inca people believed that powerful spirits lived in huacas in mountains, rivers and caves. They left offerings there, to bring good luck. Rich nobles left food or clothes. Poor people left blades of grass, drops of water – or just an eyelash.

Who wrote in pictures?
Mayan and Aztec scribes. The Mayans invented the first writing in America, using a system of picture symbols called glyphs. Mayans and Aztecs both wrote in zig-zag folding books, called codexes, using paper made from fig-tree bark.

Who were the Aztecs?
The Aztecs were wandering hunters who arrived in Mexico around AD 1200. They fought against the people already living there, built a huge city on an island in a marshy lake, and soon grew rich and strong.

Who invented chocolate?
Aztec cooks. They made a sweet, frothy chocolate drink from ground-up cocoa beans and honey, flavoured with spices. We still use a version of the Aztec name for this drink – 'chocolatl' – today.

Who was the great Feathered Serpent?
An important Aztec god – his real name was Quetzalcoatl. The Aztecs believed that one day, he would visit their homeland and bring the world to an end. Quetzalcoatl was portrayed in many Aztec drawings and sculptures. He was worshipped and feared by many other South American peoples, too.

Feathered god

Quetzalcoatl drawn by an Aztec scribe.

How did the Mayas, Aztecs and Incas lose their power?
They were conquered by soldiers from Spain, who arrived in America in the early 16th century, looking for treasure – especially gold.

Who fought the Flowery Wars?

FIERCE AZTEC SOLDIERS, ARMED WITH BOWS AND ARROWS, KNIVES AND CLUBS. During the 15th and early 16th centuries, they fought against other tribes who lived in Mexico, in battles called the Flowery Wars. The Aztecs believed that the blood of their enemies fertilized the land and enabled flowers and crops to grow. They sacrificed prisoners of war and offered their hearts to the gods.

Mayan palace, Palenque

The massive stairway leads to the royal apartments, its doorways flanked by carvings of gods and kings.

What were Mayan palaces made of?
Great slabs of stone, or sun-dried mud brick, covered with a layer of plaster, then decorated with pictures of gods and kings. Mayan temples were built in the same way, but were painted bright red.

Who lived in a circular city?

THE CITIZENS OF BAGHDAD, FOUNDED IN 762 AD BY RULER CALIPH AL-MANSUR, the most powerful Muslim of his time. He employed the best builders and architects to create a huge circular city, surrounded by strong walls. His royal palace was at the centre of the circle, with government offices and army barracks nearby. There were mosques, hospitals, schools, libraries, markets, fountains and gardens. Craftworkers and all kinds of traders lived on the outer rim of the city. Poor people and farmworkers lived outside the walls. Today the modernized city of Baghdad is the capital of Iraq.

Samarra's spiral tower

Who was the Prophet Muhammad?
A religious leader who lived in Arabia from AD 570 to 632. He taught people to worship Allah (God). Muhammad reported that he had received many revelations (messages) from God about how to lead a good life. These were written down in a holy book called the Qur'an.

What is Islam?
The religious faith taught by the Prophet Muhammad. People who follow the faith of Islam are called Muslims.

Who were the Mongols?
Tribes of nomads who roamed over the vast plains of Central Asia, tending their horses, sheep and goats. They lived in felt tents, called yurts.

Where is this spiral tower?
At Samarra, in present-day Iraq. It is a part of a mosque (place of worship) built for the caliphs of Baghdad around 848 AD. Five times a day, a muezzin (caller) climbed to the top of the tower to summon Muslim people to prayer.

When did the Mongols attack?
In AD 1206, all the separate Mongol tribes united under a warlike leader, called Temujin. He took the title Genghis Khan (supreme ruler) and set out to conquer the world. His armies destroyed Baghdad in 1258. By 1279, they controlled a vast empire, stretching from China to eastern Europe.

What were the Crusades?
A series of wars fought between Christian and Muslim soldiers for control of the area around Jerusalem (in present-day Israel), which was holy to Muslims, Christians and Jews. The Crusades began in 1096, when a Christian army attacked. They ended in 1291 when Muslim soldiers forced the Christians to leave.

Crossing the desert

Muslim merchants led camel trains laden with valuable goods across the deserts of Arabia. They carried frankincense (a perfumed gum from an Arabian tree), pearls and fine glassware.

Where was the Muslim world?
From around 700 to 1200 AD the Muslim world included southern Spain, North Africa, Northwest India, Central Asia and almost all the Middle East. It was ruled by Muslim princes and governed by Muslim laws. The scientists and scholars of the Muslim world wrote books in Arabic, and all across this vast area the ordinary people shared many traditions and beliefs.

Loose robes keep people cool in the desert heat and turbans and scarves protect against windborne sand.

Where did Muslim traders sail?
All round the Mediterranean, down the east coast of Africa, across the Indian Ocean and on to Indonesia and the lands nearby. They traded Middle Eastern silver, glass and perfumes for cloth, slaves, herbs and spices.

Who invented astrolabes?
Muslim scientists who lived and worked in the Middle East, round about 800 AD. Astrolabes were scientific instruments that helped sailors find their position when they were out of sight of land. They worked by measuring the height of the sun above the horizon.

Astrolabe

What were ships of the desert?

CAMELS BELONGING TO TRAVELLING MERCHANTS WHO LIVED IN ARABIA. They were the only animals that could survive long enough without food and water to make exhausting journeys across the hot, dry desert, laden with valuable goods to sell. They stored enough nourishment in their humps to last for ten days. Camels were smelly and bad-tempered, but they were highly prized.

Which rulers claimed descent from the Sun goddess?
The emperors of Japan. The first Japanese emperor lived around 660 BC; his descendants ruled until AD 1192. After that, army generals, called shoguns, ran the government, leaving the emperors with only religious and ceremonial powers.

Who made laws about cartwheels?
Qin Shi Huangdi, the first Chinese emperor, who united the country, made strict new laws, reformed the coinage and burned all books he disagreed with. He ruled from 221 to 207 BC, and was buried with 6,000 terracotta warriors guarding his tomb. He wanted to stop carts crashing on rutted roads, so gave orders that they should all have wheels the same distance apart. That way, they could follow the same track.

Who wrote one of the world's first novels?
Lady Murasaki, who lived at the elegant, cultured Japanese court around AD 1015. Japanese nobles loved music, poetry, painting, graceful buildings and exquisite gardens. They lived shut away from ordinary people, who had harsh, rough lives.

A pottery model of a bullock cart on the Silk Road

Carts were made of wood and woven bamboo, with strong wooden wheels.

Where did the Silk Road run?
From rich Chinese cities, across the Gobi desert, through the mountains of Central Asia to trading ports in the Middle East and around the Mediterranean Sea. European merchants travelled for years along the Silk Road to bring back valuable goods, especially silk and porcelain.

Where was the Middle Kingdom?

THE CHINESE BELIEVED THEIR COUNTRY TO BE AT THE VERY CENTRE OF THE WORLD, which is why they called it the Middle Kingdom. Certainly, for many centuries, China was one of the largest, richest and most advanced civilizations anywhere on Earth. Under the Tang and Song dynasties (ruled AD 618–1279), for example, Chinese cities like Chang'an (present-day Xi'an) and Kinsai (present-day Huangzhou) were the biggest in the world, and very prosperous. At the same time, Chinese scientists and inventors made many important discoveries, including printing, porcelain, paper-making, rockets, gunpowder, banknotes and clockwork.

Who valued honour more than life?
Japanese warriors, called samurai, who were powerful from around AD 1200. They were taught to fight according to a strict code of honour. They believed it was better to commit suicide rather than face defeat.

When was the world's first book printed?
No one knows for certain, but it was probably between AD 600 and 800, in China. The world's oldest surviving book is 'The Diamond Sutra', a collection of religious texts, also printed in China, in AD 868.

What made China so prosperous?

THE INVENTIONS OF CHINESE FARMERS AND ENGINEERS MADE THE LAND PRODUCTIVE, and this made China wealthy. In the Middle Ages, the Chinese made spectacular strides in agriculture. They dug networks of irrigation channels to bring water to the rice fields. They built machines like the foot-powered pump (below) to lift water to the fields from canals. They also worked out ways of fertilizing fruit and vegetable plots with human manure.

Ming vase

Chinese potters left clay to weather for up to 40 years before firing (baking) at very high temperatures, until it was smooth as glass.

How did China get its name?

From fine pottery and porcelain, produced by Chinese workers, which was admired and valued in many parts of the world. Chinese potters pioneered many new techniques and designs. Some of their most famous pieces were decorated with blue-and-white glazes, like this tall jar, made around AD 1350.

What was China's best-kept secret?

How to make silk. For centuries, no one else knew how. Chinese women fed silk-moth grubs on mulberry leaves, and the grubs spun thread and wrapped themselves in it, to make cocoons. Workers steamed the cocoons to kill the grubs, unwound the thread, dyed it, and wove it into cloth.

Foot-powered water pump

Men worked for hours at this endless-chain machine. It forced water to flow uphill, pushed by wooden squares, to irrigate the fields.

Who did battle in metal suits?

KINGS, LORDS AND KNIGHTS WHO LIVED IN EUROPE DURING THE MIDDLE AGES. In those days, men from noble families were brought up to fight and lead soldiers into battle. It was their duty, according to law. Around AD 1000, knights wore simple chain-mail tunics, but by around 1450, armour was made of shaped metal plates, carefully fitted together. The most expensive suits of armour were decorated with engraved patterns or polished gold.

Which Russian Tsar was terrible?
Ivan IV, who became Tsar in 1533, when he was only three years old. He was clever but ruthless, and killed everyone who opposed him. He conquered vast territories in Siberia, and passed laws turning all the Russian peasants into serfs – unfree people, like slaves.

What was the Ancien Regime?
The system of government in many parts of Europe between AD 1600 and 1800. That was when kings and queens ruled without consulting the ordinary people in their lands. The result was that royalty and nobility were very rich and powerful, while almost everyone else was powerless and poor.

Who farmed land they didn't own?
People from poor peasant families. Under medieval law, all land belonged to the king, or to rich nobles. They let the peasants live in little cottages in return for rent or for work on their land. Sometimes, the peasants protested about this arrangement, or tried to run away.

How much were war horses worth?
A knight's war horse was his most valuable possession. It cost him as much as a small private plane or a top-of-the-range luxury car today.

Which French king lost his head?
Louis XVI. Under his oppressive rule, the poor French rose up in protest. In 1789, the French Revolution began. Three years later, Louis was sent to the guillotine and beheaded.

Who was the Virgin Queen?
Elizabeth I of England, who reigned from 1556 to 1603 – at a time when many people believed that women were too weak to rule. Elizabeth proved them wrong. Under her leadership, England grew stronger. She decided not to marry, because she could not find a husband who did not want to take over her power.

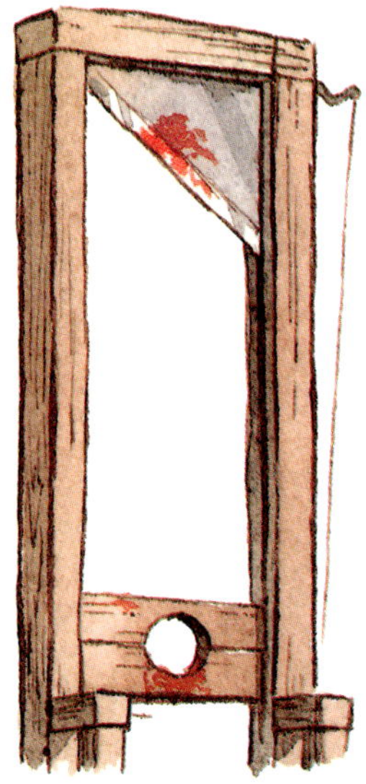

The guillotine

Who built castles and cathedrals?

KINGS, QUEENS AND RICH NOBLES WHO LIVED IN EUROPE IN THE MIDDLE AGES. The first castles were just rough wooden forts. Later, they were built of stone, and became impressive homes. They were decorated with carvings, paintings and fine furniture. Some even had flower gardens outside. Cathedrals were very big churches, in cities or towns. Merchants, master-craftsmen and other rich citizens gave money to help build them. They wanted to worship there – and also to create a beautiful building that brought honour to their town.

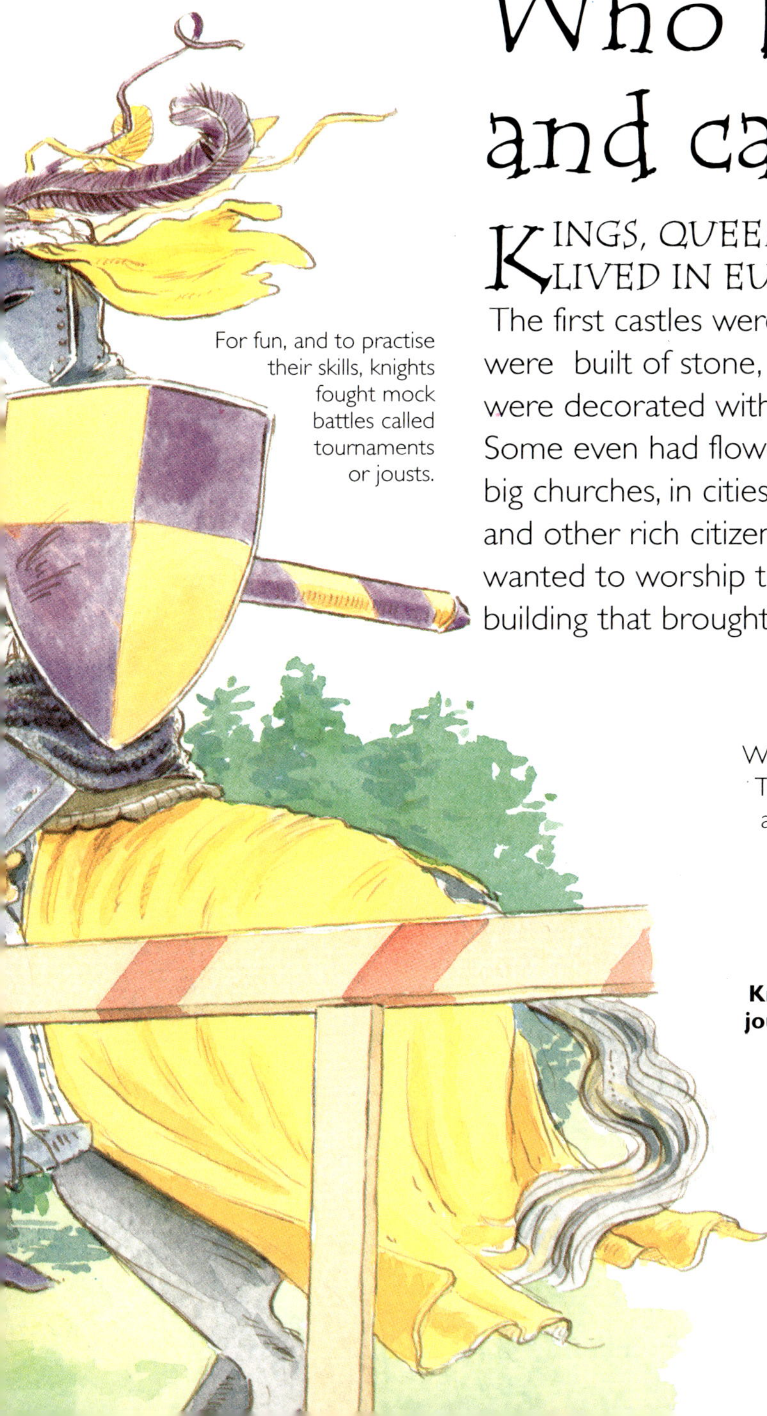

For fun, and to practise their skills, knights fought mock battles called tournaments or jousts.

Knights jousting

What job was fit for a lady?
When knights went into battle, their ladies ran the castle. They supervised the household and discussed business and politics with important guests. Some women also fought to defend their castles against attack.

When were the Middle Ages?
Some say the Middle Ages began around AD 500, others say around AD 1000. But everyone agrees that they ended round about AD 1500.

Who prayed the day away?
Monks and nuns spent a third of their lives at prayer. They promised never to marry and devoted their lives to God.

Taj Mahal

One of the most beautiful buildings in the world, the Taj Mahal, near Agra in India, was built in 1653.

Who built his wife a beautiful tomb?
Mughal emperor Shah Jehan (ruled 1627–1658). He was so sad when his wife Mumtaz Mahal died giving birth to their 14th child that he built a lovely tomb for her, called the Taj Mahal. It is made of pure white marble decorated with gold and semi-precious stones.

Who founded a new religion in India?
Guru Nanak, a religious teacher who lived in Northwest India from 1469–1539. He taught that there is One God, and that people should respect one another equally, as brothers and sisters. His followers became known as Sikhs.

Who conquered a kingdom aged only 14?

PRINCE BABUR, WHO WAS DESCENDED FROM THE GREATEST MONGOL WARRIOR GENGHIS KHAN. He captured the rich Central Asian city of Samarkand in 1497, and made it his own private kingdom. He invaded Afghanistan, and conquered northern India in 1526. Babur was a good scholar and administrator, as well as a soldier. He founded a new empire in India, and a new dynasty of rulers. They became known as the Mughals, which was the North Indian way of writing Mongols.

Grain was stored in the tall towers. The houses were made of earth and roofed with grass thatch held up on wooden poles.

Who was the Tiger King?
Tippu Sultan, king of the southern Indian state of Mysore from 1785 to 1799. Tippu means tiger, and he fought as fiercely as a tiger to defend his land against British and Mughal soldiers.

Why did British merchants go to India?
To make their fortunes! They knew that Indian goods – especially cotton cloth, drugs and dyestuffs – fetched high prices in Europe. In 1600 they set up the East India Company, to organize trade. The Company grew very rich, and had its own private army. By 1757, it controlled the richest parts of India and almost all Indian trade.

Who lived in a rose-covered palace?
The rulers of Vijayanagar, a kingdom in southern India. Their royal palace was covered in carvings of roses and lotus flowers, and surrounded by lakes and gardens. Vijayanagar was conquered by the Mughals in 1565.

How long did the Mughals rule?
For more than three centuries – from 1526 to 1858. But from around 1750, Mughal emperors were weak and powerless. The last Mughal emperor was turned off his throne when the British government took control of India after Indian soldiers working for the British East India Company rebelled in 1857.

Who swapped salt for sandalwood and gold?
Merchants from the north coast of Africa who travelled across the Sahara desert to trade with people living in the West African kingdoms of Ghana, Mali and Songhay, which were powerful from around AD 700 to 1600. Flakes of gold were found among gravel in West African rivers and streams; sweet smelling sandalwood came from tropical trees.

Who was the Great She Elephant?

This was a title of respect given to the Queen Mother in southern African kingdoms, now part of present-day Botswana and neighbouring lands. It honoured her status as mother of the king, and showed her power.

Which African city had a famous university?

Timbuktu, in present-day Mali, West Africa. The city was founded in the 11th century and became a great centre of learning for Muslim scholars from many lands. Timbuktu also had many mosques and markets, a royal palace, and a library.

Who made wonderful statues of brass and bronze?

Artists and craftworkers living in the great rainforest kingdom of Benin (part of present-day Nigeria), which was powerful from around 1400 to 1900. The statues were used to decorate the royal palace, and were placed on family altars in honour of dead ancestors.

The fortress city of Great Zimbabwe

This vast palace city was built of carefully cut and shaped stones. The Shona kings lived there with their servants and warriors.

Which kings built tall stone towers?

SHONA KINGS OF SOUTHEAST AFRICA, WHO BUILT A CITY CALLED GREAT ZIMBABWE. Zimbabwe means Stone Buildings – and the city was also a massive fortress. From inside this fortress, the Shona kings ruled a rich empire AD 1200–1600. The Shona were originally farmers, growing millet and raising cattle. Later they became skilled miners and metal workers. They traded gold, copper, iron, ivory and leather with Arab merchants living on the East African coast. In return they bought glass and fine porcelain.

Where did dhows sail to trade?

Dhows were ships built for rich merchants living in trading ports like Kilwa, in East Africa. They sailed to the Red Sea and the Persian Gulf to buy pearls and perfumes, across the Indian Ocean to India to buy silks and jewels, and to Malaysia and Indonesia to buy spices.

Did the Aboriginals always live in Australia?
No, they probably arrived there from Southeast Asia around 50,000 BC, at a time when the sea surrounding Australia was much shallower than today. Historians think they travelled in log rafts or boats made of dug-out tree trunks.

How did the Maoris cross the vast Pacific Ocean?
By sailing and paddling big outrigger canoes. They steered by studying the waves and the stars, and made maps out of twigs and shells to help themselves navigate.

Who were the first people to discover New Zealand?
The Maoris. They migrated from other Pacific Islands around AD 950 and landed on the coast of New Zealand, which had been uninhabited until then. By around AD 1400, Maori families had settled throughout the land.

What were dingoes used for?
Dingoes are a type of dog. They were brought to Australia by Indian Ocean traders around 2000 BC. They were used as guard dogs – and to keep Aboriginal people warm as they slept around campfires in the desert, which gets very cold at night.

Aboriginal hunters

Aboriginals used spears to kill kangaroos for food.

Who lives in the Australian desert?

THE ABORIGINAL PEOPLE HAVE LIVED IN THE DESERT FOR THOUSANDS OF YEARS. In that time, they have made valuable discoveries about the desert environment, and developed special survival skills. They learned how to find underground water, and to dig up nourishing roots hidden deep in the earth. They discovered which seeds, berries, grubs and animals are poisonous, and which are good to eat. They perfected the use of wild herbs in natural remedies. They found out how to use fire to scorch the earth and encourage wild food plants to grow. In addition, they invented throwing sticks called boomerangs for hunting kangaroos, and nets and traps for catching birds.

Who explored the eastern seas?
Muslim explorer Ibn Battuta, who was born in Tangiers, North Africa, sailed to India and China in the 14th century. He was followed by Cheng Ho, a Chinese admiral, who made seven long voyages between 1405 and 1433. Cheng explored the seas around India, Arabia and the east coast of Africa. He sailed south to Malayasia and Indonesia, and may even have sighted Australia.

Who arrived in America by mistake?
Italian explorer Christopher Columbus. In 1492, he sailed westwards across the Atlantic Ocean from Spain. He hoped to reach China or India, but arrived instead in America. He did not know it was there!

Which pirate became an explorer, too?
Sir Francis Drake, an English sailor who grew rich and famous by robbing Spanish ships. In his ship the 'Golden Hind', Drake made the second voyage round the world between 1577 and 1580. In 1588, Drake became a war-hero, when he led an English fleet to fight against the invading Spanish Armada.

A brief history of exploration across the oceans of the world

1304–1377 Ibn Battuta sails to India and China.
1405–1433 Cheng Ho's voyages to Africa and Indonesia.
1419 Portuguese explorers begin to sail along the west coast of Africa.
1492 Columbus sails by mistake to America.
1497 Vasco Da Gama sails round Africa to reach India.
1519–1522 Magellan's ship sails round the world.
1577–1580 Drake sails round the world.
1642 Tasman sails to Australia.
1768–1779 Captain Cook explores the Pacific.

Who sailed round the world?

THE FIRST ROUND-THE-WORLD TRIP WAS MADE BY SAILORS in the ship 'Vittoria', owned by Ferdinand Magellan, a Portuguese explorer. In 1519, he sailed eastwards from Europe, but was killed fighting in the Philippines. Most of his crew died too, from hunger or disease. A few survivors, led by sea-captain Sebastian del Cano, managed to complete Magellan's planned voyage, and returned home to Europe, weak but triumphant, in 1522.

How did sailors help science?

By observing the plants, fishes and animals as they travelled – and by bringing specimens home with them. When Captain Cook explored the Pacific Ocean he took artists and scientists with him, to study and record what they saw.

The 'Vittoria'

Magellan set off from Europe with a fleet of five ships, but only the 'Vittoria' survived.

Who lived in tents on the Great Plains?

Totem pole

Magical creatures are carved on this totem pole. It was made by skilled craftsmen in Northwest America (present-day Canada).

NATIVE AMERICAN HUNTERS, LIKE THE SIOUX/DAKOTA AND THE CHEYENNE. They spent summer and autumn moving across the wide, rolling grasslands of the Great Plains, following herds of buffalo, which they killed for meat and skins. In winter time, they camped in sheltered valleys or woods. Before Europeans settled in America, bringing horses with them, Great Plains hunters travelled vast distances on foot. They had no animals to ride – the Native American horse died out around 10,000 BC.

What stories do totem poles tell?
Native American people who lived in the forests of Northwest America carved tall totem poles to record their family's history, and to re-tell ancient legends about the powerful spirits that lived in all rocks, mountains, wild animals and trees.

Who or what were the Three Sisters?
Beans, maize and squash (pumpkin) – three essential foodcrops that Native American farmers grew wherever they could.

Who built strange shaped mounds?
The Hopewell Native American people, who lived on the banks of the Ohio River around AD 200–550. They buried their dead under huge heaps of earth, and created massive earth-mound sculptures, to honour their gods. The biggest, Great Serpent Mound, is about 400 metres (1330 ft) long.

Home on the Plains

A Native American woman and her child prepare to say goodbye to a hunter outside their tipi (tent) on the Great Plains. The hunter rides bareback – without a saddle.

Who were the first Europeans to settle in America?
Spanish missionaries, who settled in present-day Florida and California from around 1540, and French and English farmers, who built villages in present-day Virginia, on the east coast, from 1584.

Why did the Pilgrims leave home?
The Pilgrims were a group of English families with strong religious beliefs. They quarrelled with church leaders in England, and with the government, too. In 1620, they sailed for America in their ship 'Mayflower'. They wanted to build a new community, ruled by their own religious laws.

Did Native Americans live in big cities?
Yes, some of them. The people who lived in the Mississippi valley around AD 700–1200 built huge cities as centres of farming and trade. Their biggest city was called Cahokia – about 10,000 people lived there.

How did nomads move their tipis?
First, they unwrapped the skin covering of the tipi, and bundled it up. They packed up floor mats and rugs, too. Then they tied the tipi poles together to make a big A-shaped frame, called a travois, and loaded the bundles on top. The heavy travois was pulled along by women or dogs as the nomads moved from one camp to the next.

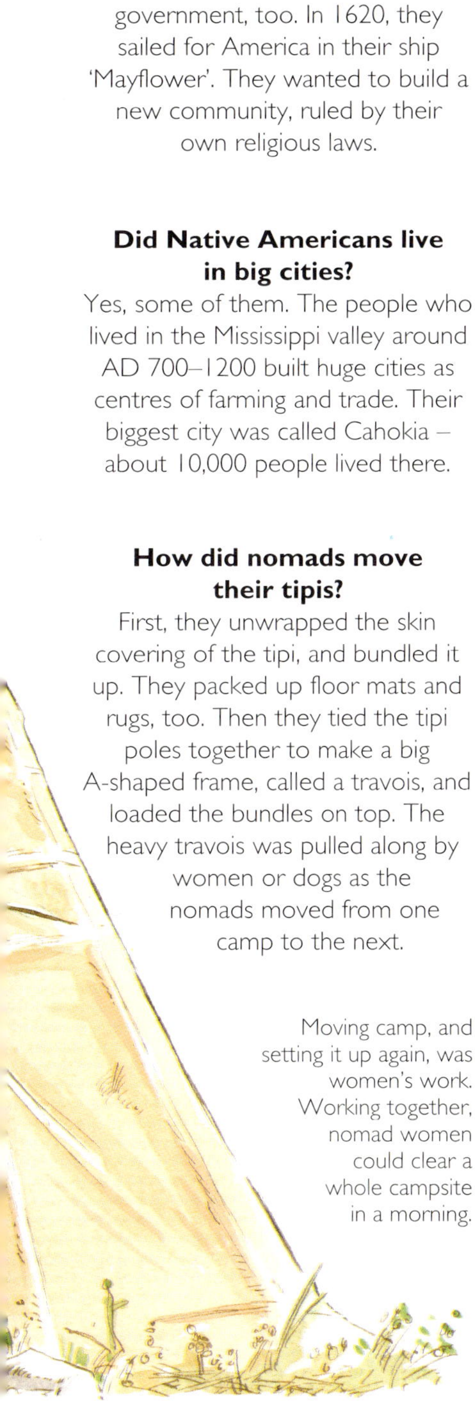

Moving camp, and setting it up again, was women's work. Working together, nomad women could clear a whole campsite in a morning.

Soldiers in the American Civil War

A Confederate soldier from the southern states, supporting slavery.

A Union soldier from the northern states, opposing slavery.

Why did a civil war break out in America?

THE AMERICAN CIVIL WAR WAS CAUSED MAINLY BY A QUARREL OVER SLAVERY. The war lasted from 1861 to 1865 and was fought between the southern and northern states of the USA. The economy of the southern states relied on black slaves shipped from Africa to work in the cotton plantations and on the farms of wealthy white owners. The northern states knew that slavery was wrong, and wanted it banned. There were also disagreements about law-making, politics and trade. After four years of heavy fighting, the northern states finally won, and most of the slaves were set free.

Who went to the Boston Tea Party?
European settlers in America attended this famous demonstration. In 1773, they poured tonnes of tea imported from Britain into the waters of Boston harbour. They were protesting against paying taxes to help the British government fund the wars it was fighting in far-away Europe. They wanted to ban all British taxes, and campaigned for the freedom to rule their own land.

When did the USA become independent?
On 4 July 1776, 13 English colonies (the land where most Europeans in America had chosen to settle) proclaimed a Declaration of Independence. In it they refused to be ruled by Britain any longer. They became a new nation – the United States of America. Britain sent troops to fight the USA and try and win the colonies back, but was defeated in 1783.

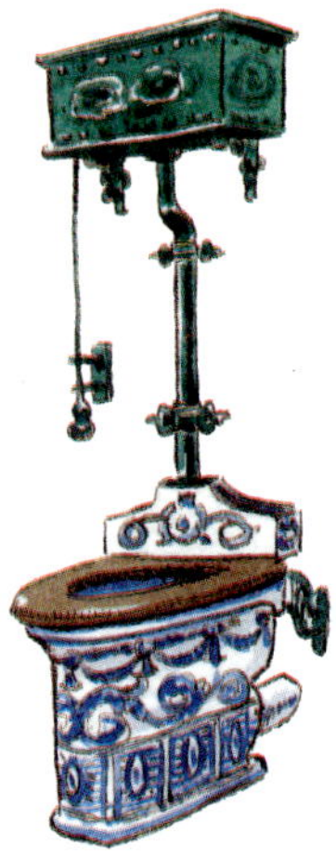

Late 19th-century lavatory

By 1900 many ordinary homes had lavatories, but only the rich could afford a polished wooden seat and an elaborately painted pottery pan like this.

Why were drains and lavatories so important?
Because without them, deadly diseases carried in sewage could spread very quickly through crowded industrial towns. Pottery-making was one of the first mass-production industries. Machines in 19th-century pottery factories produced millions of cups, plates – and lavatory pans.

What was the Industrial Revolution?

IT WAS A BIG CHANGE IN THE WAY PEOPLE WORKED AND GOODS WERE PRODUCED. It began around 1775 in Britain and spread to Belgium, Germany, northern Italy, France and – after 1850 – to Japan and the USA. Machines in huge factories replaced the craftworkers who used to make all kinds of goods slowly, one by one, at home. People had to learn new jobs operating machines that could mass-produce very large quantities of clothes, shoes, paper, metal and wooden goods more quickly and cheaply than the hand-workers could.

'The Rocket', built by George and Robert Stephenson in 1829

Who worked in the first factories?

THOUSANDS OF POOR, HUNGRY, UNEMPLOYED MEN AND WOMEN moved from the countryside to live in fast-growing factory towns. They hoped to find regular work and more pay. Wages in factories were better than those on farms, and some people enjoyed the excitement and bustle of living in a town. But working conditions in factories were often dirty and dangerous, and houses in factory towns were crowded, noisy and full of disease.

Did new industries make people rich?
They made some inventors and factory owners very rich indeed. This angered many ordinary workers, who often earned barely enough to stay alive. They joined together to form Trades Unions, to campaign for better pay and conditions.

When did the first trains run?
Horse-drawn railway wagons had been used to haul coal trucks in mines since the 1600s, but the first passenger railway was opened by George Stephenson in the north of England in 1825. Its locomotives were powered by steam. People rode standing in open carriages.

Did children lead better lives?
No. Many worked 16 hours a day in factories and down mines. Large numbers were killed in accidents with machinery, or died from breathing coal dust, cotton fibres or chemical fumes. But after 1830, governments began to pass laws to protect child workers, and conditions slowly improved.

How did railways change people's lives?
They helped trade and industry grow, by carrying raw materials to factories, and finished goods from factories to shops. They carried fresh foods from farms to cities. They made it easier for people to travel and encouraged a whole new holiday industry.

Who fought and died in the trenches?
Millions of young men during the First World War (1914–1918). Trenches were ditches dug deep into the ground. They were meant to shelter soldiers from enemy gunfire, but offered little protection from shells exploding overhead. Soon, the trenches filled up with mud, water, rats and dead bodies, and many soldiers drowned in them, or died from disease.

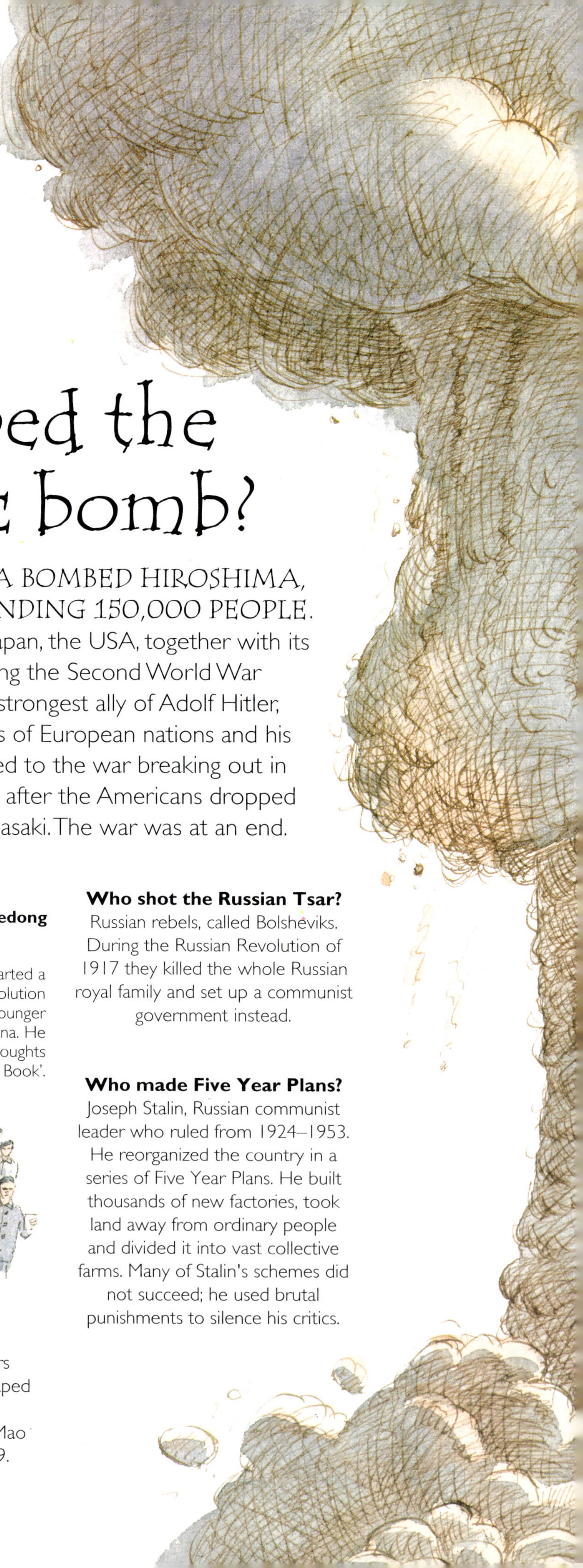

Who dropped the first atomic bomb?

ON 6 AUGUST 1945 THE USA BOMBED HIROSHIMA, JAPAN, KILLING OR WOUNDING 150,000 PEOPLE. By using this terrible new weapon on Japan, the USA, together with its allies in Britain and Russia, hoped to bring the Second World War (1939–1945) to an end. Japan was the strongest ally of Adolf Hitler, ruler of Nazi Germany. Hitler's invasions of European nations and his persecution of the Jewish people had led to the war breaking out in 1939. On 14 August Japan surrendered after the Americans dropped another atom bomb on the city of Nagasaki. The war was at an end.

Mao Zhedong

In 1966 Mao started a Cultural Revolution among the younger generation in China. He wrote down his thoughts in the 'Red Book'.

What was the Long March?
A gruelling march by Chinese communist soldiers through wild, rocky countryside in 1934. They escaped from land held by their enemies and set up a communist state of their own. They were led by Mao Zhedong, who became ruler of all China in 1949.

Who shot the Russian Tsar?
Russian rebels, called Bolsheviks. During the Russian Revolution of 1917 they killed the whole Russian royal family and set up a communist government instead.

Who made Five Year Plans?
Joseph Stalin, Russian communist leader who ruled from 1924–1953. He reorganized the country in a series of Five Year Plans. He built thousands of new factories, took land away from ordinary people and divided it into vast collective farms. Many of Stalin's schemes did not succeed; he used brutal punishments to silence his critics.

Who competed in the Space Race?
The USSR and the USA. Each tried to rival the other's achievements in space, because they hoped to prove that their nation was best. The USSR took the lead by launching the first satellite in 1957 and the first manned space flight in 1961, but America won the race by landing the first man on the Moon in 1969.

Man on the Moon

American astronaut Neil Armstrong was the first person to walk on the Moon, on 20 July 1969.

What was the Cold War?
A time of dangerous tension from 1947 to 1989 between the USA and the USSR – the two strongest nations on Earth. They had very different political systems and they distrusted and feared one another. The USA believed in freedom and big business; the USSR was communist. The superpowers never fought face to face, but they encouraged wars between smaller nations as a way of increasing their power.

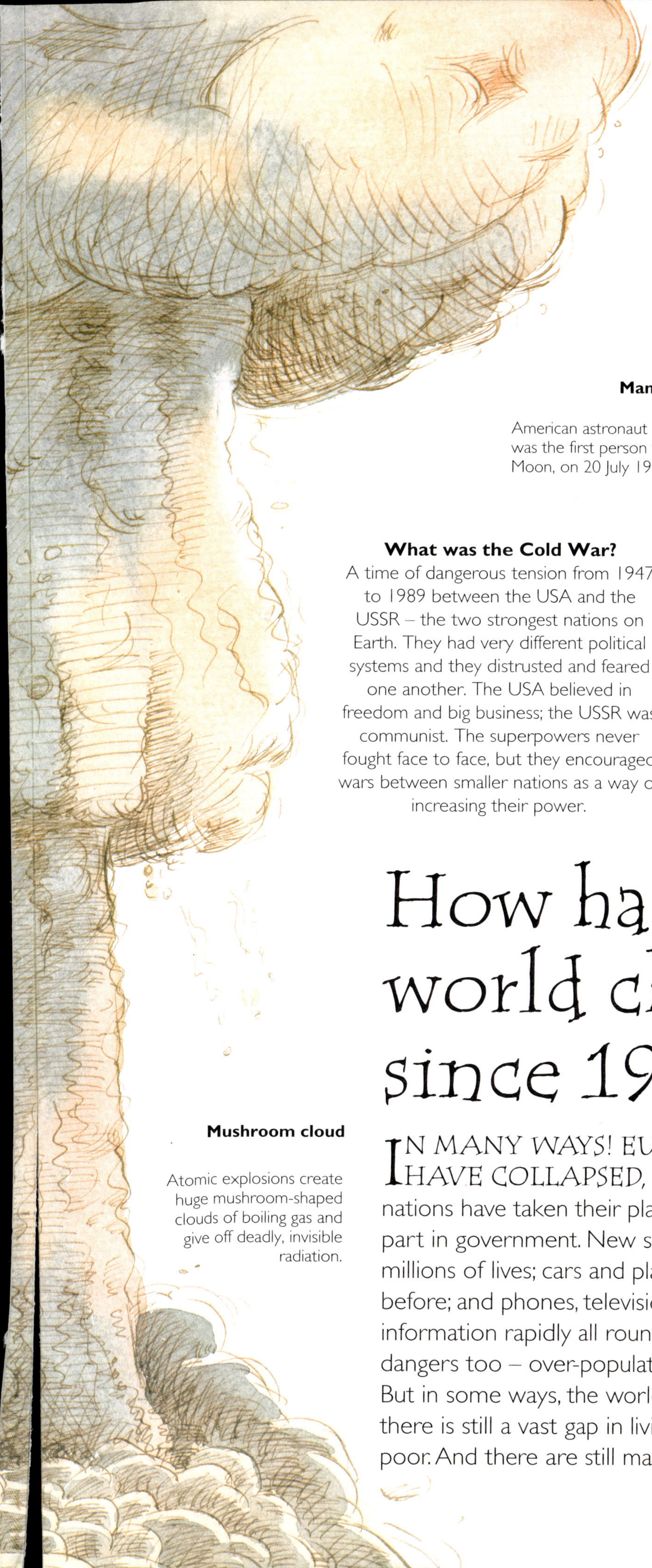

Mushroom cloud

Atomic explosions create huge mushroom-shaped clouds of boiling gas and give off deadly, invisible radiation.

How has the world changed since 1900?

IN MANY WAYS! EUROPEAN EMPIRES IN ASIA HAVE COLLAPSED, AND NEW INDEPENDENT nations have taken their place. Women now play an important part in government. New scientific knowledge has saved millions of lives; cars and planes make travel faster than ever before; and phones, televisions and computers send information rapidly all round the world. There are new dangers too – over-population, mass terrorism, and pollution. But in some ways, the world has hardly changed at all. Sadly, there is still a vast gap in living standards between rich and poor. And there are still many wars being fought.